Garfield
Large & in Charge

BY JIM DAVIS

Ballantine Books • New York

A Ballantine Books Trade Paperback Original

Copyright © 2008 by PAWS, Inc. All rights reserved.
"GARFIELD" and the GARFIELD characters are trademarks of PAWS, Inc.

Published in the United States by Ballantine Books, an imprint of The Random House Publishing Group, a division of Random House, Inc., New York.

BALLANTINE and colophon are registered trademarks of Random House, Inc.

ISBN 978-0-345-49172-5

Printed in China

www.ballantinebooks.com

9 8 7

GARFiELd
GOes to the DOGs

EVERY CAT SHOULD OWN ONE

ARF!

dOGs MAKe GOOD pETS.

DOGs TURn aROUnD THReE TimEs BeFORe LYiNG DoWN.

THEY CAN'T SLEEP UNLESS THEY'RE DIZZY

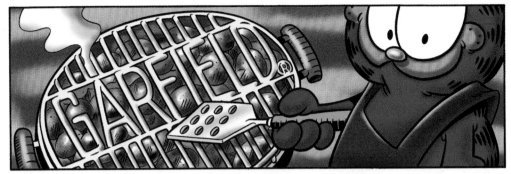

WELL, I'M ON A DIET AGAIN, AND YOU KNOW WHAT THAT MEANS...

Distributed by Universal Press Syndicate

SORRY I'M LATE!

FOOD HALLUCINATIONS

THERE WAS A TWELVE-PICKLE PILEUP IN THE KITCHEN

© 2004 PAWS, INC. All Rights Reserved.

TRAFFIC WAS BACKED UP FOR SEVERAL FLOOR TILES

JIM DAVIS 4-18

www.garfield.com

NOT VERY FILLING, BUT ALWAYS ENTERTAINING

I HAD A DREAM ABOUT FOOD

BURP

WITH ONIONS

GARFIELD, I KNOW YOU'RE ON A DIET...

BUT HOW WOULD YOU LIKE A WHOLE, ENTIRE BOWL OF FOOD?

HERE IS YOUR VEGGIE BURGER, GARFIELD

WHAT?!

ARE THE COWS ON STRIKE?!

Distributed by Universal Press Syndicate   www.garfield.com   © 2004 PAWS, INC. All Rights Reserved.   JIM DAVIS 4-19   4-20   4-21

5

HOW'S THE SALAD?

ASK IT YOURSELF. I'M NOT SPEAKING TO IT

JIM DAVIS 4-22

I'LL BE RIGHT BACK

CRINKLE

I HEARD THAT CANDY WRAPPER!

WHAT MAKES YOU THINK IT WASN'T A CELERY STALK WRAPPER?

JIM DAVIS 4-23

GARFIELD, I'VE DECIDED TO TAKE UP WOODWORKING

WHAT WOULD YOU LIKE ME TO MAKE FIRST?

LASAGNA

JIM DAVIS 4-24

6

Garfield ®

GOOD OL' GRASS...

GREEN...

www.garfield.com

SOFT... COOL...

AND WHEN YOU LIE ON IT...

© 2004 PAWS, INC. All Rights Reserved.

-THE ONLY WAY YOU CAN LOOK IS UP

LET'S HEAR IT FOR SPIRITUAL MOMENTS!

Distributed by Universal Press Syndicate

JIM DAVIS 4-25

LET THE BAD TIMES ROLL!

JIM DAVIS 4-26

JIM DAVIS 4-27

SOMETIMES I HAVE TO WONDER, GARFIELD...

WHERE IS LIFE TAKING ME?

HOW ABOUT OVER THERE, GARLIC BREATH?

JIM DAVIS 4-28

MY BACK ITCHES

GREAT NEWS, JON! YOUR PATHETIC EXISTENCE IS ABOUT TO HAVE SOME PURPOSE!

I FEEL SO FULFILLED

LOWER

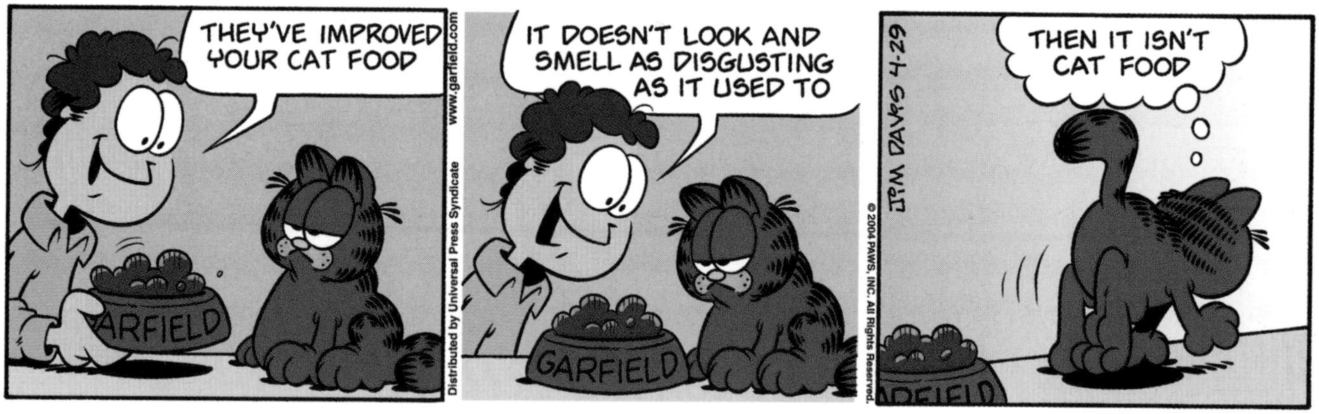
THEY'VE IMPROVED YOUR CAT FOOD
GARFIELD
www.garfield.com
Distributed by Universal Press Syndicate
IT DOESN'T LOOK AND SMELL AS DISGUSTING AS IT USED TO
GARFIELD
JIM DAVIS 4-29
© 2004 PAWS, INC. All Rights Reserved.
THEN IT ISN'T CAT FOOD

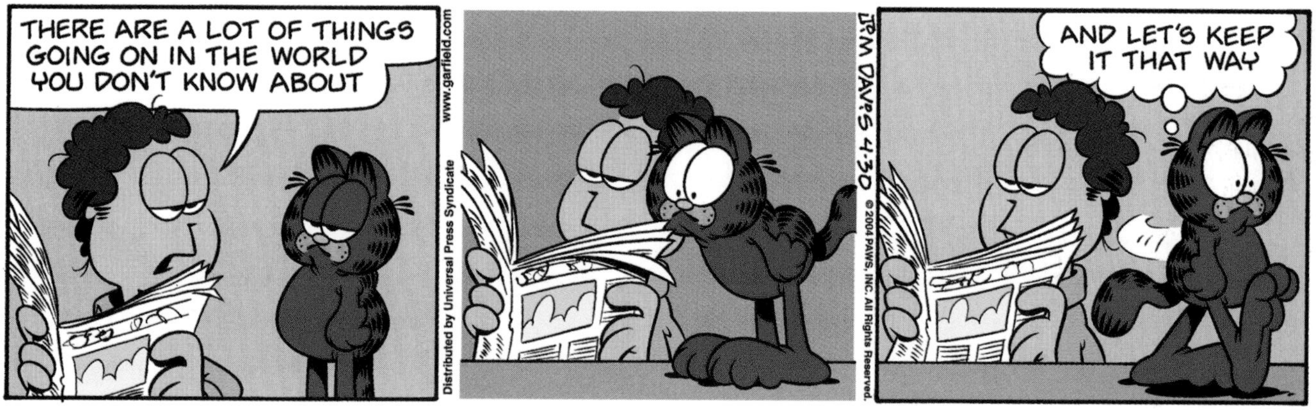
THERE ARE A LOT OF THINGS GOING ON IN THE WORLD YOU DON'T KNOW ABOUT
www.garfield.com
Distributed by Universal Press Syndicate
JIM DAVIS 4-30
© 2004 PAWS, INC. All Rights Reserved.
AND LET'S KEEP IT THAT WAY

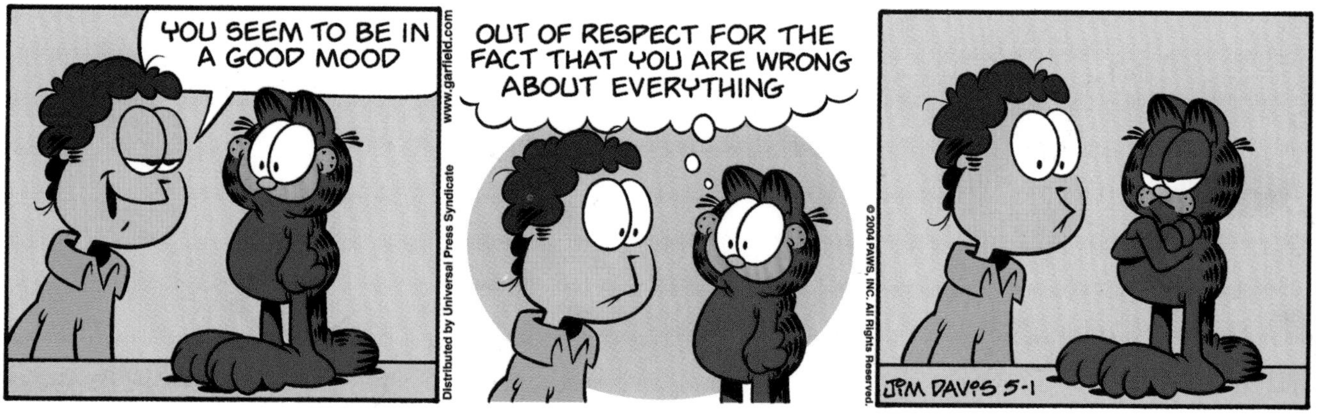
YOU SEEM TO BE IN A GOOD MOOD
www.garfield.com
Distributed by Universal Press Syndicate
OUT OF RESPECT FOR THE FACT THAT YOU ARE WRONG ABOUT EVERYTHING
© 2004 PAWS, INC. All Rights Reserved.
JIM DAVIS 5-1

GARFIELD

Z

GARFIELD! BREAKFAST!

www.garfield.com

© 2004 PAWS, INC. All Rights Reserved.

SHOOP

JiM DAViS 5-2

MORNINGS SHOULD COME EQUIPPED WITH DIMMER SWITCHES

GARFIELD

Distributed by Universal Press Syndicate

JON! LET'S HANG OUT TOGETHER!

GOLLY, IT SEEMS LIKE WE'VE ALREADY SPENT THE WHOLE DAY TOGETHER!

DING DONG

THAT'S MY STORY AND I'M STICKING TO IT

OUR NEIGHBORS ARE CIRCULATING A PETITION COMPLAINING ABOUT ALL THE ANNOYING THINGS YOU DO

I KNOW

I STOLE IT

SMACK!

JIM DAVIS 5-4

THERE ARE CLAW MARKS ON THE COUCH

WHOA! AND I JUST CLAWED THE COUCH!

THAT'S ONE SPOOKY COINCIDENCE, HUH?

JIM DAVIS 5-5

GARFIELD, I'M NOT SURE YOU CAN BE TRUSTED

WHY WOULD YOU SAY THAT?

OH, LOOK. I FOUND YOUR WALLET

JIM DAVIS 5-6

YOU'RE A BAD BOY, GARFIELD!

I CAN'T HELP IT

JIM DAVIS 5-7

SOMETIMES COUCHES JUST CRY OUT TO BE CLAWED

I'M NEVER TAKING YOU TO A FURNITURE STORE AGAIN

YOU'RE NO FUN

IT WOULD BE WRONG TO PULL ODIE'S TAIL

...AND THEN KICK HIM OFF THE TABLE

WHAT ARE YOU DOING?

MAKING A LIST

JIM DAVIS 5-8

CATNIP MOUSE

WOO-HOOO!!!

Distributed by Universal Press Syndicate

© 2004 PAWS, INC. All Rights Reserved.

www.garfield.com

JIM DAVIS 5-9

MAYBE I'LL CLAW JON

MAYBE I'LL GO GET US SOME ICE CREAM

IF ANYBODY CLAWS JON, THEY'LL HAVE ME TO ANSWER TO!

MOST OF THE EARTH'S SURFACE IS COVERED BY WATER

WHO CARES?

HOW MUCH OF IT IS COVERED BY LASAGNA?

WE CAN'T DO ANYTHING ABOUT THE PAST

BUT WE **CAN** DO SOMETHING ABOUT THE FUTURE

SOUNDS LIKE A LOT OF EFFORT TO ME

I LIKE THE FUTURE JUST THE WAY IT'S GOING TO BE

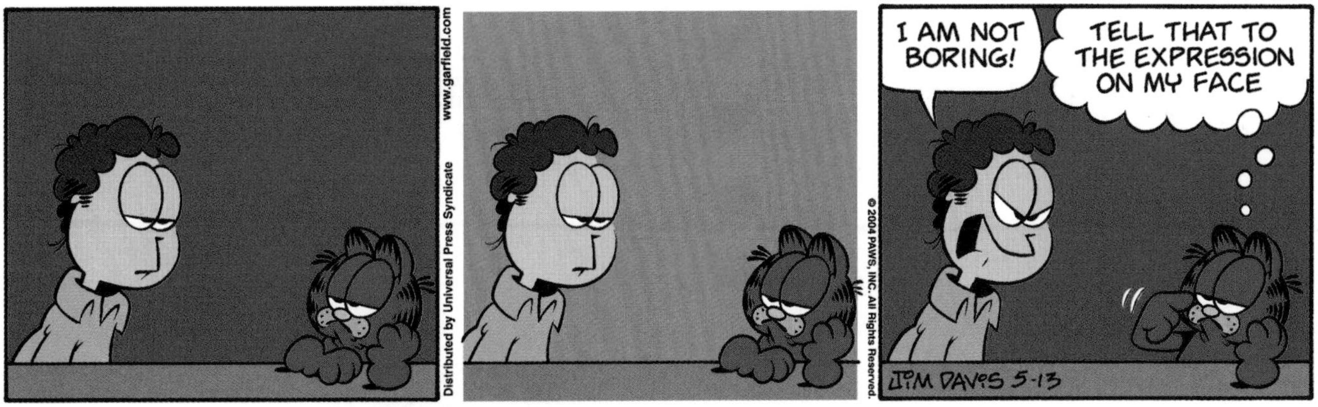
I AM NOT BORING!
TELL THAT TO THE EXPRESSION ON MY FACE
JPM DAVIS 5-13

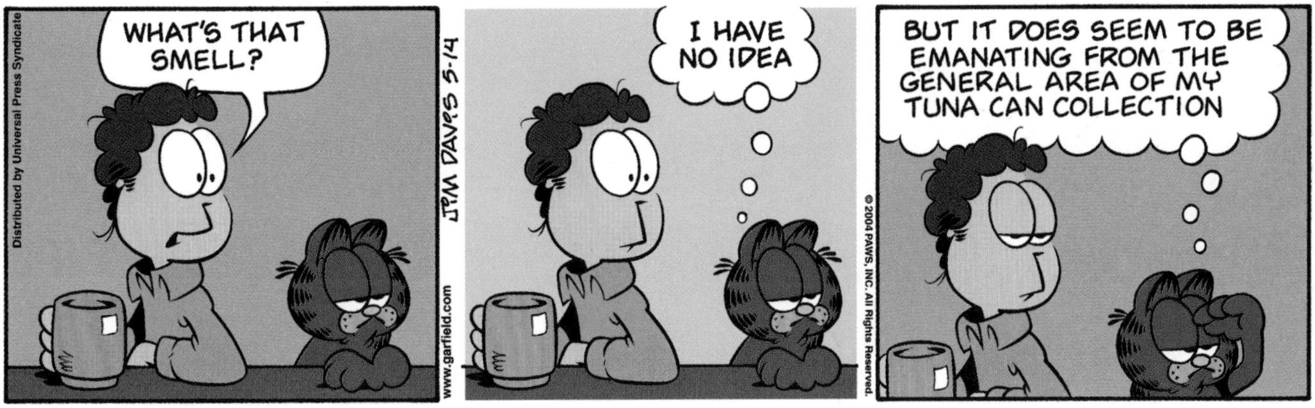
WHAT'S THAT SMELL?
I HAVE NO IDEA
BUT IT DOES SEEM TO BE EMANATING FROM THE GENERAL AREA OF MY TUNA CAN COLLECTION
JPM DAVIS 5-14

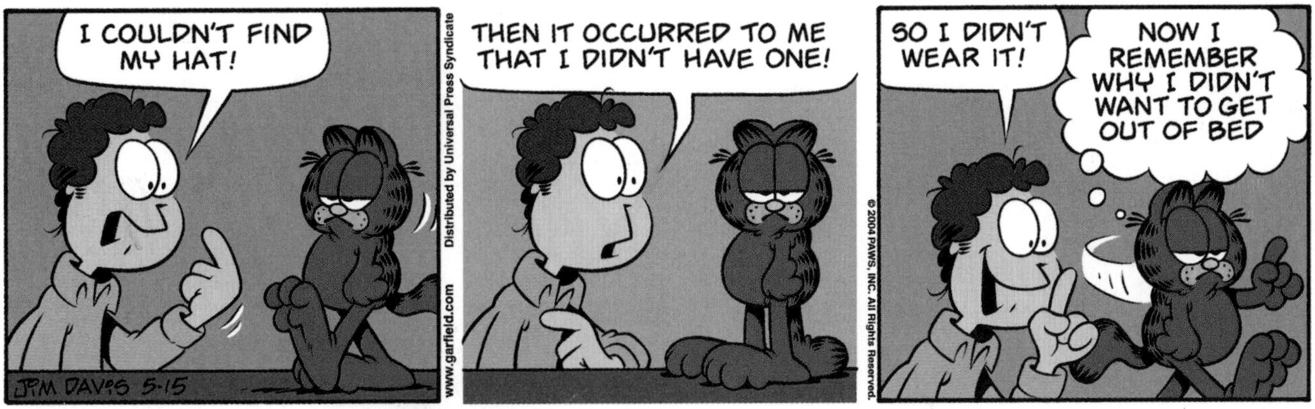
I COULDN'T FIND MY HAT!
THEN IT OCCURRED TO ME THAT I DIDN'T HAVE ONE!
SO I DIDN'T WEAR IT!
NOW I REMEMBER WHY I DIDN'T WANT TO GET OUT OF BED
JPM DAVIS 5-15

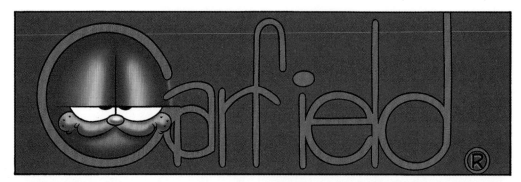

I COULD SLEEP ALL DAY

Distributed by Universal Press Syndicate

Z

Z

OH WELL...

www.garfield.com

IF AT FIRST YOU DON'T SUCCEED...

JIM DAVIS 5-16

16

YOU DON'T HAVE MANY WORRIES, DO YOU?

SURE I DO...

LIKE, CAN YOU PULL A MUSCLE BLINKING?

JIM DAVIS 5-17

SOMETIMES I LIKE TO MAKE ODIE FEEL SPECIAL!

ODIE, THERE'S NOBODY AS PECULIAR AS YOU ARE

JIM DAVIS 5-18

I'M GOING OFF TO WORK IN THE DONUT MINES

COOL!

DIG UP SOMETHING WITH ICING!

COUNT ON IT, GOOD BUDDY!

I'M DREAMING AREN'T I?

JIM DAVIS 5-19

YOU NEVER ASK ME ABOUT MY DAY

HOW WAS YOUR DAY?

I'M A SOCK PUPPET, DUMMY! WHAT DO YOU THINK IT WAS LIKE?!

IT'S AN EXTRA-LONG SPIN CYCLE FOR YOU, PAL

JIM DAVIS 5-20

AM I BOTHERING YOU?

AM I? AM I? HUH? AM I?...WELL?

JIM DAVIS 5-21

BECAUSE I'M SURE BOTHERING MYSELF

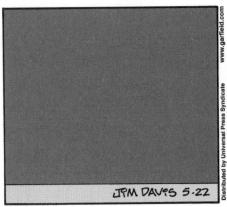
JIM DAVIS 5-22

WE NOW RETURN TO "GARFIELD MYSTERY THEATER"!

WHAT HAPPENED TO MY LUNCH?!

SOME MYSTERIES ARE BEST LEFT UNSOLVED

GARFIELD

GARFIELD!

GARFIELD!!

GARRRRRR-

FIEEEEFFELD!!!

LOZENGE?

Distributed by Universal Press Syndicate

© 2004 PAWS, INC. All Rights Reserved.

www.garfield.com

JIM DAVIS 5-23

19

YOU DON'T HAVE MUCH ENERGY

OOOKAAAY....

AND JUST HOW MUCH ENERGY DO I NEED TO ACCOMPLISH THIS?

THERE'S A SLICE OF PIZZA STUCK TO THE CEILING

AND IT APPEARS TO BE LOOSENING

THE HOUSE NEEDS CLEANING

I'M ON IT

DO YOU KNOW WHAT THIS DAY COULD USE?

KICK!

THUD

A THUD

I'M GOING TO SEE THE SIGHTS!

WHY ARE YOU STARING AT A SHADE PULL?

TO A CAT, THIS IS A SIGHT

NOBODY TELLS ME WHAT TO DO!

HAVE SOMETHING TO EAT

WELL, THIS IS A BIT AWKWARD

I JUST HEARD A JOKE

HA! HA! HA! HA! HA! HA! HA! HA!

SOMETIMES IT'S BEST TO JUST GET THOSE THINGS OVER WITH

GARFIELD

GARFIELD, I'M DEPRESSED

WHAT AN ABSOLUTE SHOCK

I HAVEN'T HAD A DATE IN MONTHS

TIME SURE FLIES WHEN YOU'RE NOT HAVING FUN

www.garfield.com

MAYBE I SHOULD GIVE KIMMY A CALL

WASN'T SHE THE ONE WHO WAS RAISED BY WOLVES?

SHE WAS RAISED BY WOLVES THOUGH, WASN'T SHE?

I CAN STILL HEAR HER BAYING AT THE MOON

© 2004 PAWS, INC. All Rights Reserved.

HELLO, KIMMY?... IT'S JON ARBUCKLE!

ASK HER IF SHE'S HAD HER SHOTS

JIM DAVIS 5-30

Distributed by Universal Press Syndicate

SOME DAYS I JUST CAN'T GET STARTED

I KNOW WHAT YOU MEAN...

1994 WAS LIKE THAT FOR ME

WOO WOO WOO!

PERSONALLY, I DON'T THINK IT'S ANY MORE THAN A TWO-WOO DAY

SIGH...

I HAVE NOTHING TO CELEBRATE

FOR THE 100TH DAY IN A ROW!

THIS DAY NEEDS IMPROVING

  I HAVE TO ADMIT, THAT'S NOT BAD

WHO KNOWS...MAYBE SOMEDAY I'LL VISIT ANOTHER PLANET  GIVE IT UP, JON  YOU WON'T BE ABLE TO GET A DATE THERE EITHER

TIME TO SEE IF MY TEETH ARE STILL SHARP ENOUGH  AAAAAH! MY LEG!  SEE YOU AGAIN FOR MY SIX-MONTH CHECKUP

GARFIELD

Distributed by Universal Press Syndicate

© 2004 PAWS, INC. All Rights Reserved.

HARF HARF HARF

HAAAACK

JIM DAV9S 6-6

HORRRF

PTOOEY
PTOOEY
PTOOEY

MORE COFFEE, BOYS?

SURE!

'BOUT TIME!

www.garfield.com

25

NO MORE OF THIS "GETTING OLDER" STUFF! FROM NOW ON I'LL...

DONK

I'LL...

OW!

JIM DAVIS 6-7

SOON I'LL BE 26 YEARS OLD

I HATE AGING

UNFORTUNATELY, AGING IS MADLY IN LOVE WITH ME

JIM DAVIS 6-8

WHAT WOULD YOU LIKE FOR YOUR BIRTHDAY, GARFIELD?

A FEATHERLESS CANARY

IT WOULDN'T TICKLE GOING DOWN

JIM DAVIS 6-9

NERMAL, YOU'RE THE NICEST CAT I KNOW

MAY I HAVE A WORD WITH YOU, NERMAL?

NOBODY'S NICER THAN I AM, IF YOU KNOW WHAT'S GOOD FOR YOU

THEY SAY THE OLDER YOU GET, THE WISER YOU GET

YOU MUST BE VERY, VERY WISE

VERY, VERY, VERY, VERY, **VERY** WISE!

I WONDER IF ANYONE WILL MISS HIM?

PEOPLE LOVE ME... KNOW WHY?

BECAUSE I'M CUTE, THAT'S WHY! AND YOU........

WELL, YOU'RE DETERIORATING

I WONDER HOW HIGH "CUTE" BOUNCES?

JIM DAVIS 6-12

BIRTHDAYS BRING YOU LOTS OF THINGS...

www.garfield.com

GRAY HAIR...

BAD EYESIGHT... CREAKY JOINTS...

© 2004 PAWS, INC. All Rights Reserved.

EAR HAIR, ACHES, PAINS, BAD TEETH...

SIGH...

Distributed by Universal Press Syndicate

AND CAKE!

6-13 JPM DAViS

28

THIS YEAR I FEEL YOUNGER THAN EVER!

NO LITTLE BIRTHDAY IS GOING TO GET ME DOWN, NO SIR...

IS IT MY IMAGINATION, OR IS THIS STRIP GETTING LONGER?

Distributed by Universal Press Syndicate   www.garfield.com   © 2004 PAWS, INC. All Rights Reserved.   JIM DAVIS 6-14

SO WHAT, SO YOU'RE GOING TO BE 26...

-TIME MARCHES ON!

COME BACK!

Distributed by Universal Press Syndicate   www.garfield.com   © 2004 PAWS, INC. All Rights Reserved.   JIM DAVIS 6-15

I'M NOT GETTING OLDER, I'M GETTING BETTER

JIM DAVIS 6-16

-EVERY DAY IN EVERY WAY

AND I'M GONNA GROW WINGS AND I'M GONNA FLY, TOO

Distributed by Universal Press Syndicate   www.garfield.com   © 2004 PAWS, INC. All Rights Reserved.

AGE IS A STATE OF MIND

WITH A HEALTHY DOSE OF DENIAL

I'M NOT SHOWING MY AGE

NOT FOR YOU OR ANYONE ELSE

SIGH...26...ANOTHER BIRTHDAY...ANOTHER YEAR...ANOTHER...

ANOTHER...

WHAT WAS I JUST THINKING ABOUT?

30

www.Garfield.com

JON! JON!

www.garfield.com

MAN, IS THIS EMBARRASSING

I COMPLETELY FORGOT WHAT I WAS GOING TO SAY!

© 2004 PAWS, INC. All Rights Reserved.

Distributed by Universal Press Syndicate

NOW I REMEMBER! YOUR CAR IS ON FIRE

JIM DAVIS 6-20

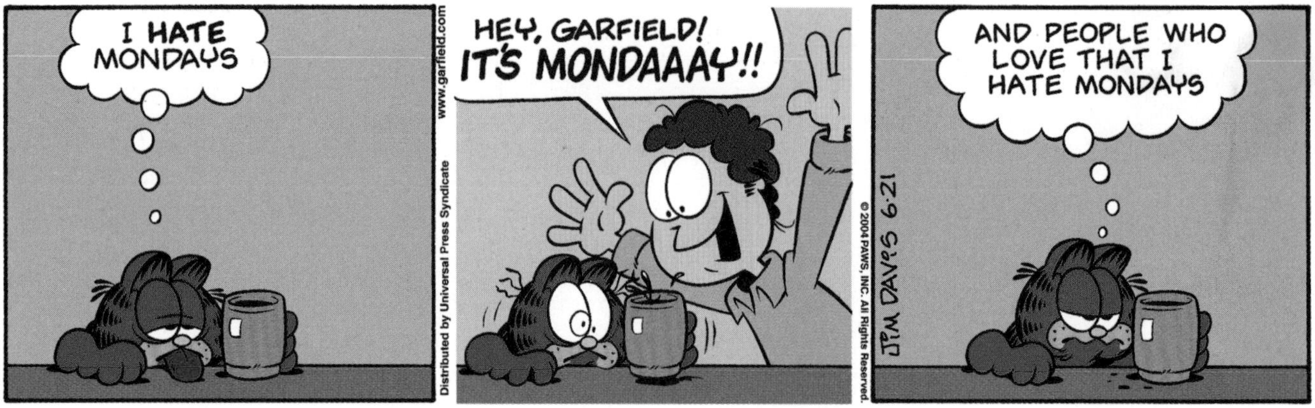
I HATE MONDAYS
HEY, GARFIELD! IT'S MONDAAAY!!
AND PEOPLE WHO LOVE THAT I HATE MONDAYS
JIM DAVIS 6-21
Distributed by Universal Press Syndicate www.garfield.com
© 2004 PAWS, INC. All Rights Reserved.

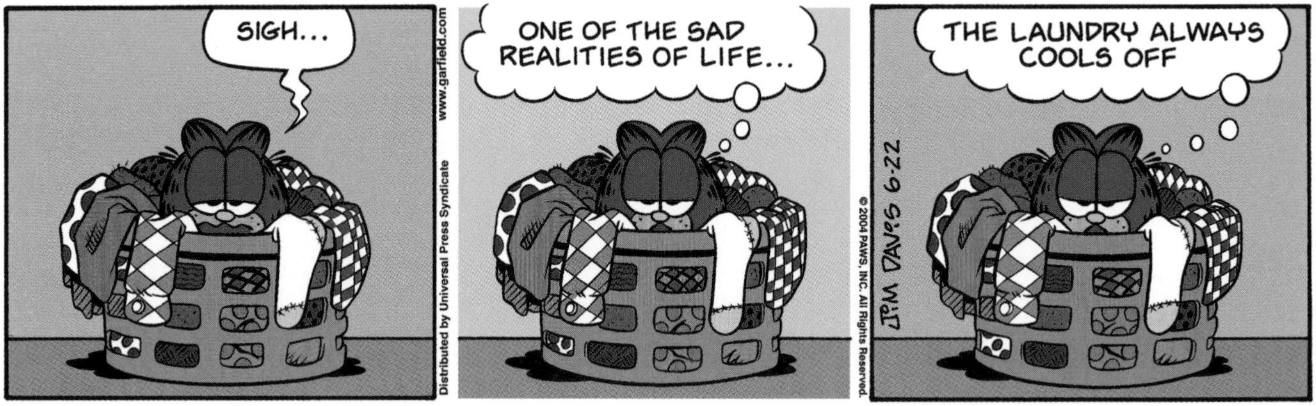
SIGH...
ONE OF THE SAD REALITIES OF LIFE...
THE LAUNDRY ALWAYS COOLS OFF
JIM DAVIS 6-22
Distributed by Universal Press Syndicate www.garfield.com
© 2004 PAWS, INC. All Rights Reserved.

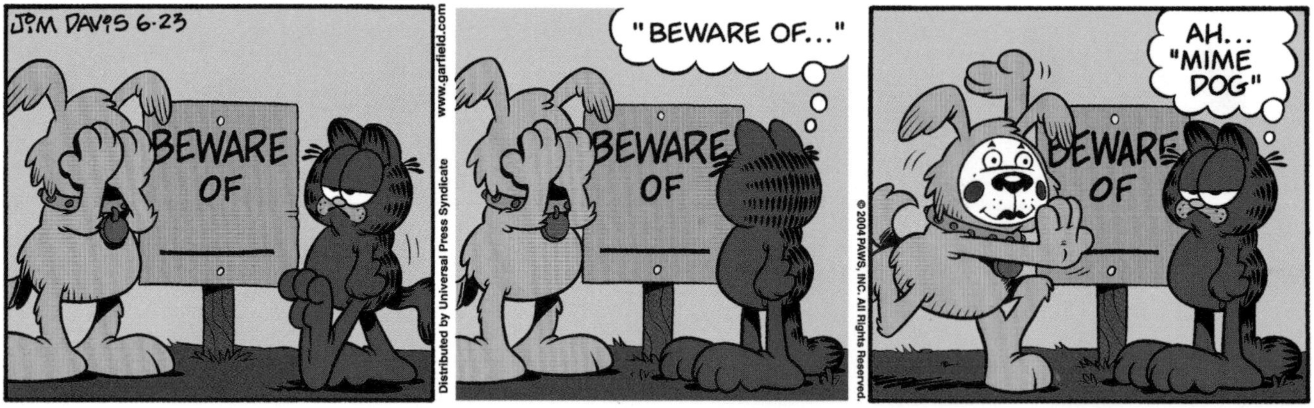
JIM DAVIS 6-23
BEWARE OF
"BEWARE OF..."
AH... "MIME DOG"
Distributed by Universal Press Syndicate www.garfield.com
© 2004 PAWS, INC. All Rights Reserved.

Z

SUPPERTIME!

YOU FELL ASLEEP HANGING ON THE SCREEN DOOR AGAIN, DIDN'T YOU?

HOW'D YA GUESS?

JIM DAVIS 6-24

OTHER ANIMALS PLAY. OTHER ANIMALS FROLIC

JIM DAVIS 6-25

WE NEED TO MAKE SOME CHANGES AROUND HERE!

YOU'RE RIGHT!

BUT HOW DO WE CHANGE ALL THOSE OTHER ANIMALS?

I RENTED A VIDEO, GARFIELD

IT HAS EVERYTHING! ACTION, ADVENTURE...

AND A GREAT SOUND TRACK!

"THE POLKA NINJAS"

JIM DAVIS 6-26

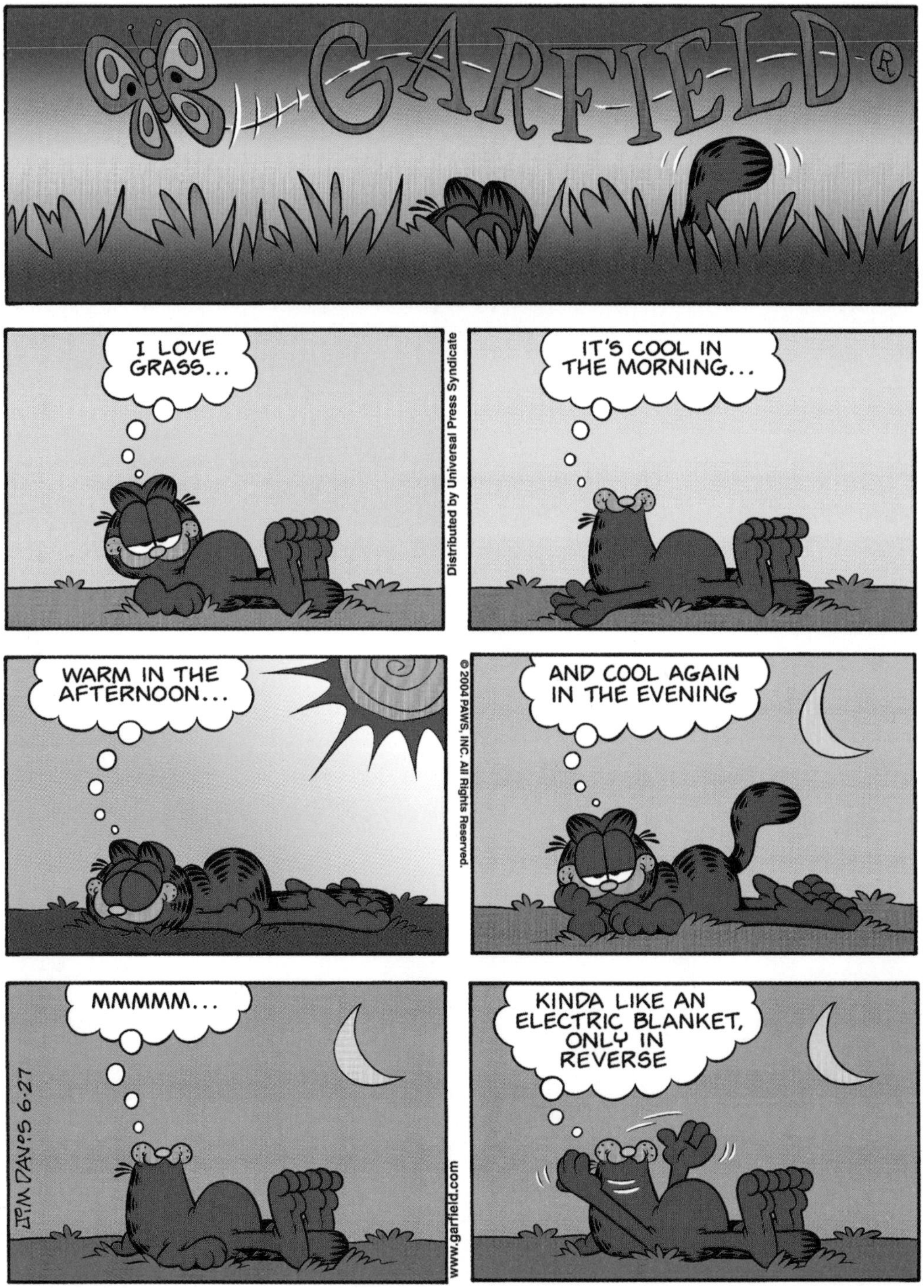
GARFIELD®
I LOVE GRASS...
Distributed by Universal Press Syndicate
IT'S COOL IN THE MORNING...
WARM IN THE AFTERNOON...
© 2004 PAWS, INC. All Rights Reserved.
AND COOL AGAIN IN THE EVENING
MMMMM...
JIM DAVIS 6-27
www.garfield.com
KINDA LIKE AN ELECTRIC BLANKET, ONLY IN REVERSE

I'VE HAD A REALLY GREAT DAY TODAY!

HOW ABOUT YOU?

OH, GARFIELD

YEAH. ASK HIM HOW HIS DAY HAS BEEN

I'M GOING TO GET YOU!

HELP! HELP!

I'M NOT BUYING IT, GUYS

I TOLD YOU WE SHOULD BE FACING THE SAME WAY

OKAY, ALREADY!

AND THAT'S WHAT CHASING MICE SHOULD LOOK LIKE!

I NOTICE YOU DIDN'T CATCH HIM

GO ON

MICE RULE!

HA! HA! HA!
I LOST A BET

I DECLARE THIS HOUSE MOUSE FREE!

WHOA! CHEESE HAS LEGS!

DO YOU MIND?!

SORRY

UH, GARFIELD?
HE'S TAKING A SHOWER

GARFIELD

DIG DIG

DIG DIG DIG

DIG DIG DIG DIG DIG

ODIE!!!

WELL, I GUESS NOT EVEN ODIE IS PERFECT

JIM DAVIS 7-4

www.garfield.com

© 2004 PAWS, INC. All Rights Reserved.

Distributed by Universal Press Syndicate

IT'S MONDAY...

THE SCREWS ON THAT CHANDELIER NEED...

TIGHTENING

SAVE ME! IT'S A GIANT MEATBALL FROM OUTER SPACE!

NEVER FEAR! THE MEATBALLINATOR IS HERE!

I HATE WAKING UP

JIM DAVIS 7-6

WHAT'S YOUR PROBLEM?

MY PROBLEM?

I ONLY GET TO HAVE ONE?

JIM DAVIS 7-7

WHY DON'T BIRDS LIKE ME?

BECAUSE YOU EAT THEM, YOU IDIOT!

I CAN LIVE WITH THAT

JIM DAVIS 7-8

ICE CUBES DOWN YOUR PANTS!

YAAAHHH! HA!HA! HA!HA!

NOW MY SODA IS WARM

JIM DAVIS 7-9

I WANT YOU TO DO NOTHING ALL DAY

JIM DAVIS 7-10

IS THIS SOME KIND OF TRICK?

39

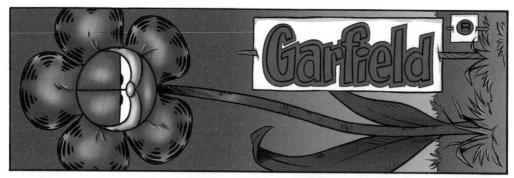

THIS WINDOW IS FILTHY

I CAN'T SEE A THING

I KNEW THAT

www.garfield.com

© 2004 PAWS, INC. All Rights Reserved.

Distributed by Universal Press Syndicate

JIM DAVIS 7-11

40

IT'S A BEAUTIFUL DAY AT THE STADIUM...

FOR THE WORLD DRINKING-OUT-OF-THE-TOILET CHAMPIONSHIP!

LAP LAP LAP LAP

NEVER LET A DOG PICK WHAT YOU WATCH

HERE WE SEE A TYPICAL DOG CHASING A SQUIRREL

AND NOW THE DOG HAS CORNERED THE SQUIRREL

HERE WE SEE THE DOG TRYING TO REMOVE A PINE CONE FROM UP HIS NOSE

DISGRACEFUL

TODAY IN THE NEWS, A GIANT METEOR STRUCK EARTH, DESTROYING ALL LIFE

WHAT?... WHAT'S THAT?

OOPS, I GUESS THAT DIDN'T HAPPEN

YOU GOTTA CHECK THOSE SOURCES, BUCKO

JIM DAVIS 7-12 © 2004 PAWS, INC. All Rights Reserved. Distributed by Universal Press Syndicate www.garfield.com

JIM DAVIS 7-13 © 2004 PAWS, INC. All Rights Reserved. www.garfield.com Distributed by Universal Press Syndicate

JIM DAVIS 7-14 © 2004 PAWS, INC. All Rights Reserved. www.garfield.com Distributed by Universal Press Syndicate

41

THE BOLIVIAN TREE FROG LIVES IN...

BORING

CLICK

THIS IS THE POLICE! WE HAVE YOU SURROUNDED!

AH

PUT DOWN THE BOLIVIAN TREE FROG!

OKAAAY...

I BELIEVE THAT TELEVISION VIEWERS ARE SMARTER THAN PEOPLE WHO READ BOOKS

WHY IS THAT?

YOU CAN'T CHANGE A BOOK WITH A REMOTE, NOW CAN YOU?

GOOD POINT

CLICK CLICK

I HAVE THIS DOWN TO A SCIENCE...

CLICK CLICK

I AVOID THE SHOWS, AND ONLY SEE COMMERCIALS!

CLICK CLICK

JIM DAViS 7-15 © 2004 PAWS, INC. All Rights Reserved.
JIM DAViS 7-16 © 2004 PAWS, INC. All Rights Reserved.
JIM DAViS 7-17 © 2004 PAWS, INC. All Rights Reserved.
www.garfield.com Distributed by Universal Press Syndicate

42

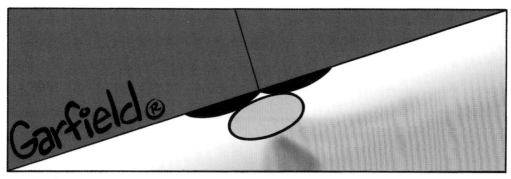

Garfield®

I'M DOWN

DISTRESSED, DEPRESSED, AND DOWN IN THE DUMPS

© 2004 PAWS, INC. All Rights Reserved.

GULP

SNATCH

Distributed by Universal Press Syndicate

NEVER UNDERESTIMATE THE POWER OF POSITIVE DONUTS!

JIM DAVIS 7-18

www.garfield.com

43

I HAVE THE URGE TO EXERCISE
WHEW! THANK GOODNESS IT PASSED
JIM DAVIS 7-19
Distributed by Universal Press Syndicate www.garfield.com
© 2004 PAWS, INC. All Rights Reserved.

STOP BOTHERING ME!
OKAY, YOU CAN BOTHER ME A LITTLE, BUT ONLY IF FOOD IS INVOLVED
JIM DAVIS 7-20
Distributed by Universal Press Syndicate www.garfield.com
© 2004 PAWS, INC. All Rights Reserved.

DARN IT, GARFIELD! WHEN I SPEAK, PAY ATTENTION!
THAT'S QUITE ENOUGH
ARE YOU DONE? MAY I QUIT NOW?
JIM DAVIS 7-21
Distributed by Universal Press Syndicate www.garfield.com
© 2004 PAWS, INC. All Rights Reserved.

CATS ALWAYS KNOW WHEN IT'S TIME FOR DINNER

WE MOUNT MINIATURE CLOSED-CIRCUIT VIDEO CAMERAS IN THE BOTTOMS OF OUR FOOD DISHES

AH! THE KITCHEN; WHERE THE FOOD IS!

AH! THE KITCHEN; WHERE THE FOOD USED TO BE!

GARFIELD

YES?

DON'T TEASE ODIE!

WHAT?

WHERE WOULD HE GET AN IDEA LIKE THAT?

JIM DAVIS 7-22
JIM DAVIS 7-23
JIM DAVIS 7-24

45

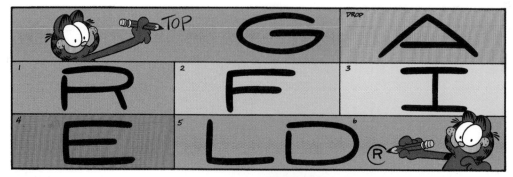

GARFIELD

TOP DROP

OH, NO! I'M LOSING MY HAIR!

MY DAD'S BALD. DOC BOY DOES A COMB-OVER!

www.garfield.com

NOW I'LL NEVER GET A WOMAN!

YAAAAH!

© 2004 PAWS, INC. All Rights Reserved.

TODAY, A BALD SPOT...

TOMORROW, A MOHAWK!

Distributed by Universal Press Syndicate

JPM DAVIS 7-25

46

ALLOW ME TO INTRODUCE A CLOSE, DEAR, AND PERSONAL FRIEND...

...THIS PORK CHOP

GET BACK HERE!

WHO WAS THAT GUY?

INTERCEPTION!

I'D LIKE TO HAVE SOMETHING DIFFERENT FOR DINNER

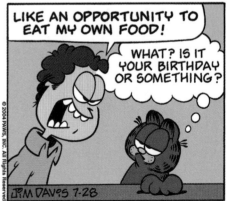
LIKE AN OPPORTUNITY TO EAT MY OWN FOOD!

WHAT? IS IT YOUR BIRTHDAY OR SOMETHING?

47

BURP

THAT WAS UNNECESSARY

YOU WOULDN'T SAY THAT IF YOU'D JUST EATEN THREE LUNCHES

JIM DAVIS 7-29

MMM...

GULP

AH, THAT SHOULD HOLD ME UNTIL I'M ABLE TO MOVE AGAIN

JIM DAVIS 7-30

DO YOU EVER GET CRAVINGS FOR CERTAIN FOODS?

BOY, I DO

RIGHT NOW, I COULD REALLY GO FOR SOMETHING EDIBLE

JIM DAVIS 7-31

48

GARFIELD

HERE I AM!

THE CENTER OF THE UNIVERSE!

BASK IN THE WONDER THAT IS ME!

BUT DON'T OVERDO IT

TRY TO KEEP FROM GETTING OVEREXCITED AND HYPERVENTILATING

WILL YOU BE LEAVING SOON?

OH, VERY WELL, BASK AWAY!

JIM DAVIS 8-1

www.garfield.com

© 2004 PAWS, INC. All Rights Reserved.

Distributed by Universal Press Syndicate

49

JON SAYS I SHOULD "SEIZE THE DAY!"

THERE'S ONLY ONE PROBLEM...

I CAN'T REACH IT FROM HERE

I'M SAVING MONEY BY CUTTING MY OWN HAIR!

YOU MUST BE SAVING MILLIONS!

I AM A MAN OF DIGNITY

OH, SURE

SINCE I HID HIS WAX LIPS

50

I PUT ON RUNNING SHOES...

JOGGING SHORTS, AND A SWEAT BAND

THAT'S ENOUGH EXERCISE FOR TODAY

HAH-LOOOOOOOO ELL-ENNNNN

CLICK

DANG. SHE SAW RIGHT THROUGH MY SUAVE ACCENT

I THOUGHT YOU WERE YODELING

YAAAAHHHHH!

YA-

SLAP

THANKS

RECURRING PORCUPINE PETTING ZOO NIGHTMARE

51

Garfield

YOU KNOW, IF I WERE YOU...

www.garfield.com

SLEEPING ALL DAY... EATING LIKE A PIG...

BEING WAITED ON HAND AND FOOT...

© 2004 PAWS, INC. All Rights Reserved.

NOT LISTENING TO A THING I SAY...

Distributed by Universal Press Syndicate

JIM DAVIS 8-8

WOW... I WISH I WERE YOU

TAKE A NUMBER

BAD WEB DAY

DO TELL

© 2004 PAWS, INC. All Rights Reserved.
Distributed by Universal Press Syndicate www.garfield.com
JIM DAVIS 8-9

SWAT ME QUICK. I'M IN A HURRY

SWAT!

HOW'S THAT?

THANK YOU. THAT FREES UP THE REST OF MY DAY

© 2004 PAWS, INC. All Rights Reserved.
Distributed by Universal Press Syndicate www.garfield.com
JIM DAVIS 8-10

TWANG!

THUD!

DIET TIME

YOU SHOULD TALK!

© 2004 PAWS, INC. All Rights Reserved.
Distributed by Universal Press Syndicate www.garfield.com
JIM DAVIS 8-11

53

IS THIS WHERE THE SPIDER CONVENTION IS BEING HELD?

YUP

Smack!

JIM DAVIS 8-12

HI THERE!

GO AWAY!

LET'S PLAY!

I CAN'T WIN

JIM DAVIS 8-13

I WAS BORED

REEEALLY BORED

JIM DAVIS 8-14

54

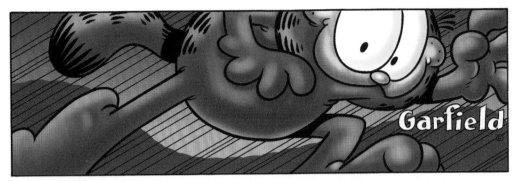

Garfield

RING

HELLO?...

Distributed by Universal Press Syndicate

HELLO? HELLO? HELLO?

IS ANYBODY THERE?

© 2004 PAWS, INC. All Rights Reserved.

THERE'S NOBODY THERE

WELL THEN, I GUESS I'LL TALK

HE'S A LONELY, LONELY MAN

JIM DAVIS 8-15

www.garfield.com

55

WHO WANTS TO HELP ME DO NOTHING?

NOT ME

I'D PROBABLY END UP DOING ALL THE WORK

AND NOW, TO READ SOME DOG POETRY, HERE'S ODIE!

YIP! YIP! YIP! YIP! YIP! YIP! YIP! YIP! YIP! YIP! YIP! YIP!

YIP! YIP...

HEY! NO LIMERICKS!

I THINK I'LL CLAW A LARGE STRANGER

OUCH!

IS THAT YOUR CAT?

NO

AM SO!

56

YAWN

JIM DAVIS 8-19

I WON'T SAY THAT WAS A LONG NAP, BUT...

WHAT YEAR IS IT?

I KNOW YOU!

I'M GOING OUT IN SEARCH OF LOVE!

WE WILL NEVER SEE JON AGAIN

JIM DAVIS 8-20

STOP STARING AT ME!

IT'S GOOD THAT WE HAVE THESE LITTLE DISCUSSIONS

JIM DAVIS 8-21

57

SIGH...

YOU NEVER PAY ANY ATTENTION TO ME...

Distributed by Universal Press Syndicate

SO I'M NOT SPEAKING TO **YOU** ANYMORE!

© 2004 PAWS, INC. All Rights Reserved.

www.garfield.com

DID YOU **HEAR** ME?!!

JIM DAVIS 8-22

58

YOU'RE LATE!

BAT

-AND YOUR FOLLOW-THROUGH NEEDS WORK!

NAG, NAG, NAG

JIM DAVIS 8-23

BAT

"HELLO FROM THE FLOOR... WISH YOU WERE HERE"

JIM DAVIS 8-24

HEY, GARFIELD

YO, YARN. WHAT'S UP?

NOT MUCH. JUST HANGING WITH MY COUSIN...

JIM DAVIS 8-25

HE'S A SPOOL OF THREAD

THERE IS A FAMILY RESEMBLANCE

59

JIM DAVIS 8-26
BINK BINK BINK
Distributed by Universal Press Syndicate
www.garfield.com

BINK BINK
© 2004 PAWS, INC. All Rights Reserved.

WHERE HAVE YOU...
IN THE HOT TUB, OKAY?!
BINK BINK

Distributed by Universal Press Syndicate

JIM DAVIS 8-27
www.garfield.com
YOU KNOW, EVEN BALLS OF YARN NEED CONDITIONER AFTER SHAMPOOING
I KNOW! I KNOW!
© 2004 PAWS, INC. All Rights Reserved.

JIM DAVIS 8-28
www.garfield.com
Distributed by Universal Press Syndicate
?

SNIFF SNIFF SNIFF

?
DOGS DON'T UNDERSTAND BALLS OF YARN
© 2004 PAWS, INC. All Rights Reserved.

60

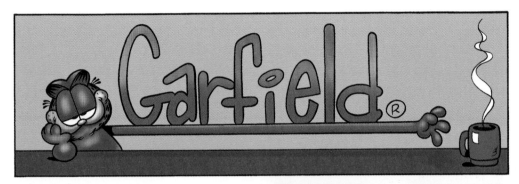

Garfield

YAWN

www.garfield.com

Z

© 2004 PAWS, INC. All Rights Reserved.

Z

Z

Distributed by Universal Press Syndicate

THE GOOD SPOTS ARE ALWAYS TAKEN

Z

JIM DAVIS 8-29

61

Distributed by Universal Press Syndicate   www.garfield.com   © 2004 PAWS, INC. All Rights Reserved.

62

WHEW!...IT SURE IS HOT

IT'S NOT SO MUCH THE HEAT, IT'S THE HUMIDITY

HE HAD THAT COMING

I'VE GOTTA FIND A WAY TO COOL OFF

ARE THOSE FROZEN PEAS?! THEY'RE ALL THE RAGE THIS SEASON

I'VE DISCOVERED A NEW WAY TO BEAT THE SUMMER HEAT

TURN UP THE AIR CONDITIONING!
WHOP!
POO!

Garfield®

www.garfield.com

JIM DAVIS 9-5

© 2004 PAWS, INC. All Rights Reserved.

Distributed by Universal Press Syndicate

SCHTONK

WATER?

IF YOU PLEASE

64

THE FLAG MOUSE WAS ACTUALLY A NICE TOUCH

JIM DAVIS 9-6

GOOD WORK, GARFIELD! BE EVER VIGILANT!

HEY! HEY! HEY!

DON'T TURN THE PAGE YET!

IF YOU'RE GOING TO READ OVER MY SHOULDER, READ FASTER!

JIM DAVIS 9-7

JIM DAVIS 9-8

WOULDN'T YOU HAVE A BETTER CHANCE OF CATCHING THE MOUSE IF YOU ACTUALLY CHASED HIM?

I'M COUNTING ON HIS PULLING UP LAME

EEK! A MOUSE!

COME ON. IT'S HIS BIRTHDAY

I'M TIRED

THEN HAVE A SEAT

PERHAPS I'VE BEEN TOO LAX ON THIS CAT-MOUSE THING

GARFIELD! CATCH THE MOUSE!

I WILL

BUT, BECAUSE I'M SUCH A GREAT SPORT, I'M GIVING HIM A HEAD START

ABOUT A TWO-WEEK HEAD START

BONK!

GARFIELD

WHO WANTS A HUG?

SOMEBODY?

ANYBODY?

NOBODY?

www.garfield.com

© 2004 PAWS, INC. All Rights Reserved.

Distributed by Universal Press Syndicate

JIM DAVIS 9-12

TIME TO EXPLORE THE OUTER REACHES OF MY UNIVERSE

GRRR
ODIE HAS SOMETHING CORNERED

GRRR

GRRR
IT'S THE CORNER

THERE'S SURELY SOMETHING ON WORTH WATCHING
CLICK CLICK CLICK

CLICK CLICK CLICK CLICK CLICK

IT'S THE ALL-LASAGNA CHANNEL!
THE MOTHER LODE!

Jim Davis 9·16

© 2004 PAWS, INC. All Rights Reserved.

 IT WAS SO STRANGE...MY DATE POSSESSED THE ABILITY TO BECOME INVISIBLE!

 UH, JON... ONE MINUTE SHE WAS THERE AND, THE NEXT MINUTE...

 SHE DITCHED YOU POOF

JIM DAVIS 9·17

 I WONDER IF THEY'LL MAKE A MOVIE ABOUT MY LIFE SOMEDAY

 ABSOLUTELY!

 BUT MORE LIKE A SOCK PUPPET SHOW

JIM DAVIS 9·18

69

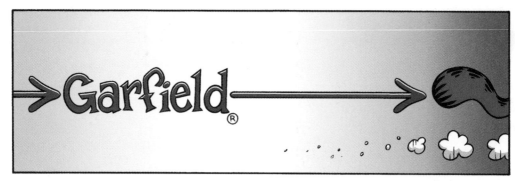

HMMM...

MAYBE JON'S RIGHT

...I SHOULD GET OUTDOORS MORE OFTEN

JIM DAViS 9-19

70

NAP TIME

THUD

JIM DAViS 9-20

YOU'RE PATHETIC

Z

AHHHHHHHH

THE NAP...

BEDTIME'S APPETIZER

JIM DAViS 9-21

SHOES

SHOES

BUNK BEDS

SHOES

JIM DAViS 9-22

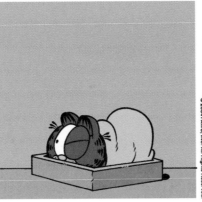

NAPS ARE ALWAYS MORE FUN WHEN THEY'RE SNUCK

JIM DAVIS 9-23

CLICK

JIM DAVIS 9-24

WHAT IF I WERE TO JUST LIE HERE FOREVER...

JIM DAVIS 9-25

AND NEVER GET UP AGAIN?

WHAT ARE YOU DOING?

THINKING HAPPY THOUGHTS

DINNER, BREAKFAST, AND LUNCH...

www.garfield.com

BREAKFAST, DINNER, AND LUNCH...

LUNCH, DINNER, AND BREAKFAST?...

Distributed by Universal Press Syndicate

BREAKFAST, LUNCH, AND DINNER!

© 2004 PAWS, INC. All Rights Reserved.

JIM DAVIS 9-26

IF IT AIN'T BROKE, DON'T FIX IT!

73

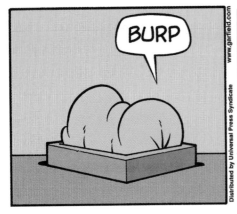
BURP

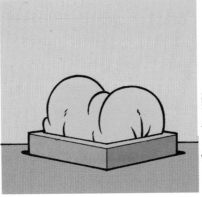

GASP!!!

HAVE A COUPON FOR A FREE CHEESEBURGER!

OKAY!

HEY! THIS HAS EXPIRED!

LOOK, GARFIELD!

SCARY, HUH?

SCARY? YOU'RE JUST WEARING A GROCERY SACK!

I'M AN EMPTY GROCERY SACK!

EMPTY?!

I'VE BEEN LYING HERE FOR 83 HOURS AND 17 MINUTES WITHOUT MOVING A MUSCLE

YES! ONLY 10 SECONDS AWAY FROM MY PERSONAL BES...

NUTS

JIM DAVIS 9-30

ELLEN, WHEN YOU SAY HURTFUL THINGS TO ME, I JUST WANT TO CURL UP AND WITHER AWAY

SHE'S SAYING HURTFUL THINGS

SO WITHER ALREADY

JIM DAVIS 10-1

TODAY IS A TEENSE LESS BORING THAN YESTERDAY

PARTY ON

JIM DAVIS 10-2

www.garfield.com
Distributed by Universal Press Syndicate
© 2004 PAWS, INC. All Rights Reserved.

75

TIME TO GET UP

YUP. GOTTA GET UP RIGHT NOW...

YESSIR-REEDY-DEEDY-DO... UP AND AT 'EM...

WHAT ARE YOU DOING?

FOOLING MYSELF

JIM DAVIS 10-3

76

GARFIELD! DID YOU EAT ALL THREE OF THOSE CAKES I BAKED?!

JIM DAViS 10-4

NOPE

TWO AND A HALF

GARFIELD...

JIM DAViS 10-5

YOU'VE BEEN EATING IN BED AGAIN, HAVEN'T YOU?

SO, SHERLOCK, WHAT TIPPED YOU OFF?

RIIIING!

HELLO?

NO, NO... IT'S ALL RIGHT

JIM DAViS 10-6

THAT WAS THE TITANIC. THEY SPOTTED AN ORANGE ICEBERG

I WONDER IF YOU FLOAT?

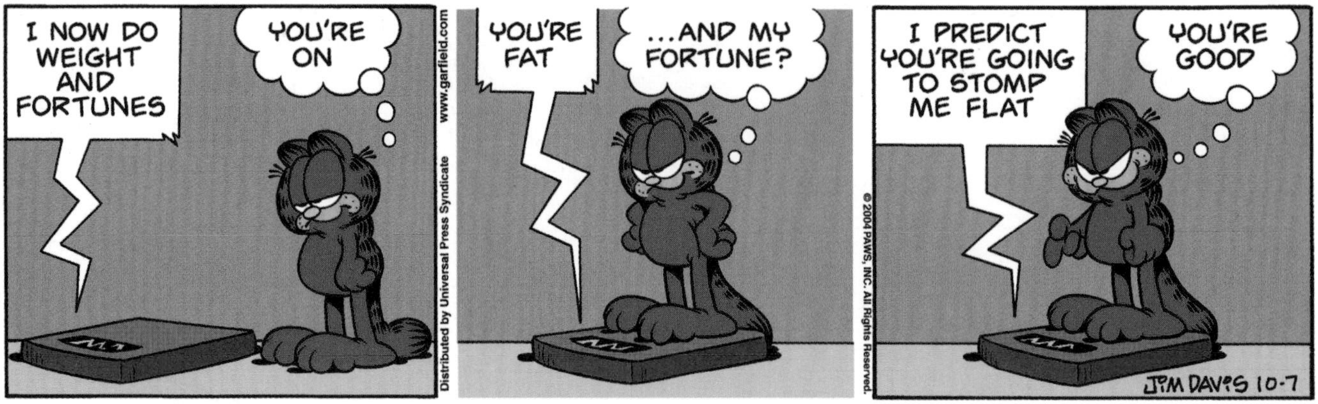
I NOW DO WEIGHT AND FORTUNES
YOU'RE ON
YOU'RE FAT
...AND MY FORTUNE?
I PREDICT YOU'RE GOING TO STOMP ME FLAT
YOU'RE GOOD
JIM DAVIS 10-7
Distributed by Universal Press Syndicate www.garfield.com
© 2004 PAWS, INC. All Rights Reserved.

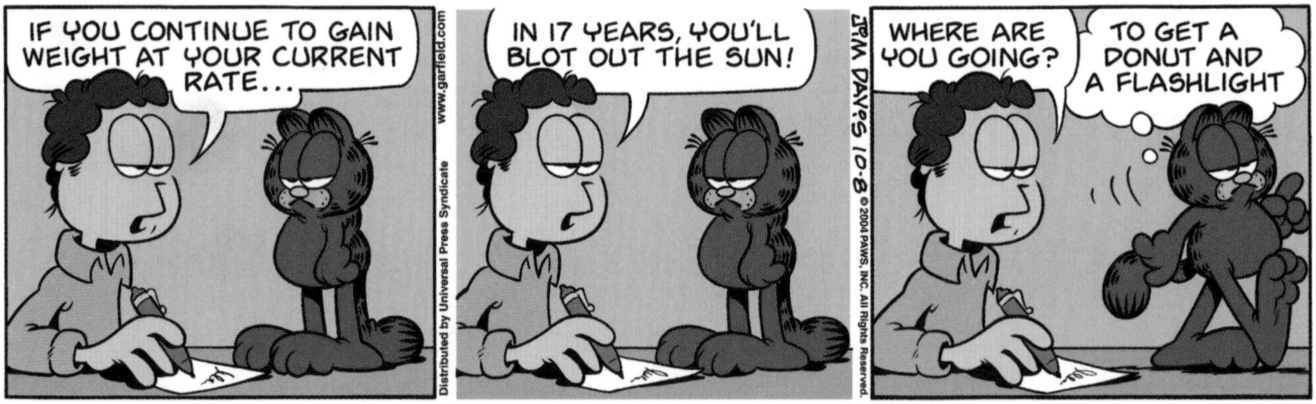
IF YOU CONTINUE TO GAIN WEIGHT AT YOUR CURRENT RATE...
IN 17 YEARS, YOU'LL BLOT OUT THE SUN!
WHERE ARE YOU GOING?
TO GET A DONUT AND A FLASHLIGHT
JIM DAVIS 10-8
Distributed by Universal Press Syndicate www.garfield.com
© 2004 PAWS, INC. All Rights Reserved.

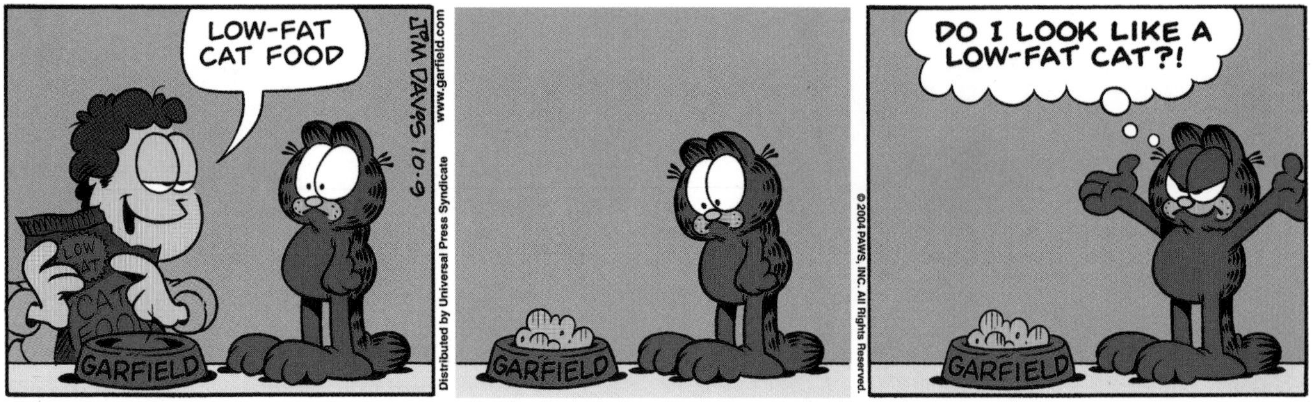
LOW-FAT CAT FOOD
GARFIELD
DO I LOOK LIKE A LOW-FAT CAT?!
JIM DAVIS 10-9
Distributed by Universal Press Syndicate www.garfield.com
© 2004 PAWS, INC. All Rights Reserved.

GARFIELD

HAVE A SALAD... HAVE A SALAD...

HAVE A SALAD...

Distributed by Universal Press Syndicate

HAVE A SALAD...

AHEM...

© 2004 PAWS, INC. All Rights Reserved.

HAVE A SALAD

THERE'S JUST NO RIGHT WAY TO SAY THAT TO HIM

www.garfield.com

JIM DAVIS 10-10

79

IF YOU CLOSE YOUR EYES, YOU CAN PRETEND THIS LETTUCE IS CHOCOLATE CAKE

IF YOU CLOSE YOUR EYES, I CAN HAVE REAL CHOCOLATE CAKE!

HEY, JON, CHECK OUT MY NEW DIET!

MUNCH MUNCH GULP

DID YOU NOTICE I CHEWED BEFORE I SWALLOWED?

HOW'S THE DIET GOING? HEY!

SOMEBODY OUT THERE'S EATING!

I WITHDRAW THE QUESTION BACON!

JIM DAVIS 10-11
JIM DAVIS 10-12
JIM DAVIS 10-13

Distributed by Universal Press Syndicate
www.garfield.com
© 2004 PAWS, INC. All Rights Reserved.

80

HOW'S THE DIET GOING?

GREAT!

I'VE CUT OUT SNACKS

I DID, HOWEVER, HAVE ELEVEN LUNCHES

I'VE EATEN ALL THE DONUTS...

NOW THEY CAN'T TEMPT ME TO CHEAT ON MY DIET

FLAWLESS LOGIC, IF EVER I'VE HEARD IT!

ARE YOU HAVING A GOOD TIME?

BECAUSE I'M NOT!

SPLOT

WAIT. THAT WAS KIND OF FUN

JIM DAVIS 10-14

JIM DAVIS 10-16

Distributed by Universal Press Syndicate

www.garfield.com

© 2004 PAWS, INC. All Rights Reserved.

GAR-FIELD ®

BURP

HI

WHOA

SAY AREN'T YOU THE INVISIBLE MAN?

NO, I'M NOT

HE'S SHORTER THAN I AM

HE'S ONLY ABOUT THIS TALL

OH, YEAH

BUT DON'T FEEL BAD. A LOT OF PEOPLE CONFUSE US

I THINK I'LL WAKE UP NOW

Distributed by Universal Press Syndicate

© 2004 PAWS, INC. All Rights Reserved.

www.garfield.com

JIM DAVIS 10-17

WHY ARE CATS SO MYSTERIOUS?

ALLOW ME TO EXPLAIN BY WAY OF AN INTERPRETIVE DANCE

WHY IS A DOG'S NOSE SO COLD?

LET'S FIND OUT

AH-HA...

GONG

WHERE DID YOU GET THE GONG?

SPANKY'S HOUSE OF ALL THINGS DINNER

GARFIELD

83

CATS ARE VERY CLEAN ANIMALS

THEY CLEAN THEMSELVES WITH THEIR TONGUES

BUT NOT YOU!

WE'RE OUT OF CONDITIONER

GARFIELD, I THINK THAT GIRL DOWN THE COUNTER IS LOOKING AT ME!

NO SHE ISN'T

I THINK SHE WANTS TO MEET ME!

NO SHE DOESN'T

I MAY HAVE BEEN MISTAKEN

YES, YOU WERE

I'M SO BORED I CAN'T BELIEVE IT

NOT ME

I CAN BELIEVE IT

84

I CAN SLEEP ANYWHERE

Z

Z

SEE?

WHOOPS

Z

© 2004 PAWS, INC. All Rights Reserved.

Distributed by Universal Press Syndicate

www.garfield.com

JIM DAVIS 10-24

WOW!

LOOK AT THAT BIG, FAT, ORANGE—

PUMPKIN

HMMM, JUST LIKE ODIE...

THE LIGHT'S ON, BUT NOBODY'S HOME

...THAT MONSTER COULD BE ANYWHERE!

...HE COULD EVEN BE RIGHT BEHIND—

HI, GUYS... CUE THE BLOODCURDLING SCREAMS

JIM DAVIS 10-25

JIM DAVIS 10-26

JIM DAVIS 10-27

86

LARRY, DON'T! ...DON'T GO IN THERE!

I MUST GO IN THERE, MARGARET!

BRAVE, LARRY

AAAAGGGHHH!

BRAVE, STUPID, LARRY

TONIGHT WE'RE SPEAKING WITH A BIG, FAT, CREEPY MONSTER

GLAD TO BE HERE

SO, WHERE DO YOU LIVE?

UNDER YOUR BED

UHHHH...

AND AREN'T YOU A LITTLE OLD TO BE WEARING BUNNY SLIPPERS?

SWEET DREAMS

WE'RE SPEAKING TODAY WITH AN ACTUAL VAMPIRE

GOOD MORNING, SIR

THANK YO- ...MORNING?

MORNING?!!

THEY JUST MIGHT WANT TO DRAW THOSE BLINDS

BOO!

PARDON?

BOO. I'M A GHOST

YOU DON'T SAY

OH, YES. I'M QUITE FRIGHTENING

NO, YOU'RE NOT

I'M NOT?

NOT EVEN CLOSE

ARE YOU SURE?

I FIND YOU VERY PLEASANT

I WISH I WERE DEAD

I'M NOT SURE HOW TO BREAK THIS TO YOU, PAL

JIM DAVIS 10-31

88

AMBITION!

DRIVE, FORTITUDE, GUMPTION, DETERMINATION...

I'VE ALWAYS WANTED TO SAY THOSE WORDS

JIM DAVIS 11-1

TIME TO TAKE A BREAK, ODIE

OUR BREAKS ARE SO LONG, OUR BREAKS NEED BREAKS

JIM DAVIS 11-2

AH... AH...

CHOO!

SO, WOULD YOU LIKE SOME TOAST?

NOT IN THIS LIFETIME

JIM DAVIS 11-3

89

SOMETIMES I SLEEP SO MUCH I CAN'T TELL IF IT'S DAY OR NIGHT

SOMETIMES I EAT SO MUCH I CAN'T TELL IF I'M HUNGRY OR FULL

IGNORANCE IS BLISS

OH, ELLEN...

MY LOVE FOR YOU IS LIKE AN ENDLESS VOID...

WAIT! WRONG SIMILE!

THAT'S THE ONE ABOUT YOUR HEAD

SACK TIME

Z

JIM DAVIS

GARFIELD

JUST LOOK AT THIS...

WHY DO DOGS ALWAYS NEED "BEWARE" SIGNS?

Distributed by Universal Press Syndicate

WE CATS DON'T NEED SIGNS...PEOPLE JUST KNOW...

WOW... YOU'RE RIGHT

© 2004 PAWS, INC. All Rights Reserved.

JIM DAVIS 11-7

www.garfield.com

I WANNA SIGN!

SMACK!

POO!

THERE ARE THINGS IN LIFE WE JUST HAVE TO ADMIT WE CAN'T CONTROL

LIKE YOU

YEAH, I'M A REAL FORCE OF NATURE

HEY, I KNOW I'M FAT... SO WHAT?

I'M FAT, AND I'M BEAUTIFUL!

NARCISSISM...USE IT OR LOSE IT

JIM DAVIS 11-9

SAY, GOOD LOOKIN'

YOU LOOK FABULOUS!

HEY, MIRRORS NEED LOVE, TOO

JIM DAVIS 11-10

92

OH, GEEZ

I NEED A HAIRCUT BAD

TRY SHEDDING, IT'S CHEAPER!

JIM DAViS 11-11

I THOUGHT I WAS GOING TO SEIZE THE DAY...

BUT THE DAY SEIZED ME INSTEAD

POOR JON

LIFE'S A SALAD BAR, AND HE JUST KEEPS SMACKING HIS FOREHEAD ON THE SNEEZE GUARD

JIM DAVIS 11-12

SO, HOW WAS YOUR DAY?

BETTER THAN YOURS

JIM DAVIS 11-13

93

GARFiELd
GOes to thE DOGS

NOTHING LIKE CHASING YOUR TAIL TO GET THE OL' HEART PUMPING!

DOgS ENJOy eXeRCiSE.

BUT **NOT** WORSE THAN HIS BREATH

A DOG's bARK iS WorsE THAN hIS BITe.

It's a party online—and YOU'RE invited!

GARFIELD.COM

News
Get the latest scoop on everyone's favorite media darling!

Fun & Games
Tons of arcade fun for everyone. Wanna play?

Comics
Read the daily comic or browse the vault for a blast from the past!

PostCards
Stay connected! Send animated greetings to all your online buds.

STRIPS, SPECIALS, OR BESTSELLING BOOKS... GARFIELD'S ON EVERYONE'S MENU.

Don't miss even one episode in the Tubby Tabby's hilarious series!

GARFIELD AT LARGE ....(#1) 978-0-345-44382-3
GARFIELD GAINS WEIGHT ....(#2) 978-0-345-44975-7
GARFIELD BIGGER THAN LIFE ....(#3) 978-0-345-45027-2
GARFIELD WEIGHS IN ....(#4) 978-0-345-45205-4
GARFIELD TAKES THE CAKE ....(#5) 978-0-345-44978-8
GARFIELD EATS HIS HEART OUT........(#6) 978-0-345-46459-0
GARFIELD SITS AROUND
   THE HOUSE..(#7) 978-0-345-46463-7
GARFIELD TIPS THE SCALES ....(#8) 978-0-345-46909-0
GARFIELD LOSES HIS FEET.................(#9) 978-0-345-46467-5
GARFIELD MAKES IT BIG ....(#10) 978-0-345-46468-2
GARFIELD ROLLS ON ....(#11) 978-0-345-47561-9
GARFIELD OUT TO LUNCH.................(#12) 978-0-345-47562-6
GARFIELD FOOD FOR THOUGHT......(#13) 978-0-345-47563-3
GARFIELD SWALLOWS HIS PRIDE....(#14) 978-0-345-91386-9
GARFIELD WORLDWIDE ....(#15) 978-0-345-91754-6
GARFIELD ROUNDS OUT ....(#16) 978-0-345-35388-7
GARFIELD CHEWS THE FAT..............(#17) 978-0-345-35956-8
GARFIELD GOES TO WAIST ....(#18) 978-0-345-36430-2
GARFIELD HANGS OUT......................(#19) 978-0-345-36835-5
GARFIELD TAKES UP SPACE ....(#20) 978-0-345-37029-7
GARFIELD SAYS A MOUTHFUL ....(#21) 978-0-345-37368-7
GARFIELD BY THE POUND.................(#22) 978-0-345-37579-7
GARFIELD KEEPS HIS CHINS UP ......(#23) 978-0-345-37959-7
GARFIELD TAKES HIS LICKS..............(#24) 978-0-345-38170-5
GARFIELD HITS THE BIG TIME ....(#25) 978-0-345-38332-7
GARFIELD PULLS HIS WEIGHT..........(#26) 978-0-345-38666-3
GARFIELD DISHES IT OUT.................(#27) 978-0-345-39287-9
GARFIELD LIFE IN THE FAT LANE .....(#28) 978-0-345-39776-8
GARFIELD TONS OF FUN...................(#29) 978-0-345-40386-5
GARFIELD BIGGER AND BETTER......(#30) 978-0-345-40770-2
GARFIELD HAMS IT UP ....(#31) 978-0-345-41241-6
GARFIELD THINKS BIG......................(#32) 978-0-345-41671-1

GARFIELD THROWS HIS
   WEIGHT AROUND ....(#33) 978-0-345-42749-6
GARFIELD LIFE TO THE FULLEST.....(#34) 978-0-345-43239-1
GARFIELD FEEDS THE KITTY ....(#35) 978-0-345-43673-3
GARFIELD HOGS THE SPOTLIGHT ...(#36) 978-0-345-43922-2
GARFIELD BEEFS UP ....(#37) 978-0-345-44109-6
GARFIELD GETS COOKIN' ....(#38) 978-0-345-44582-7
GARFIELD EATS CROW ....(#39) 978-0-345-45201-6
GARFIELD SURVIVAL OF
   THE FATTEST......................................(#40) 978-0-345-46458-3
GARFIELD OLDER AND WIDER..........(#41) 978-0-345-46462-0
GARFIELD PIGS OUT ....(#42) 978-0-345-46466-8
GARFIELD BLOTS OUT THE SUN ......(#43) 978-0-345-46615-0
GARFIELD GOES BANANAS ....(#44) 978-0-345-91346-3

DVD TIE-INS

GARFIELD AS HIMSELF...............................978-0-345-47805-4
GARFIELD HOLIDAY CELEBRATIONS 978-0-345-47930-3
GARFIELD TRAVEL ADVENTURES 978-0-345-48087-3

AND DON'T MISS...

GARFIELD AT 25: IN DOG YEARS
   I'D BE DEAD 978-0-345-45204-7
GARFIELD'S JOKE ZONE/INSULTS..............978-0-345-46263-3
GARFIELD FAT CAT 3-PACK/ VOL. 1 978-0-345-46455-2
GARFIELD FAT CAT 3-PACK/ VOL. 2 978-0-345-46465-1
GARFIELD FAT CAT 3-PACK/ VOL. 13 978-0-345-46460-6
SEASON'S EATINGS: A VERY MERRY
   GARFIELD CHRISTMAS 978-0-345-47560-2
GARFIELD'S GUIDE TO EVERYTHING 978-0-345-46461-3
ODIE UNLEASHED! 978-0-345-46464-4
GARFIELD'S BOOK OF CAT NAMES...........978-0-345-48516-8
THE GARFIELD JOURNAL..........................978-0-345-46469-9
LIGHTS, CAMERA, HAIRBALLS!:
   GARFIELD AT THE MOVIES 978-0-345-49134-3

New larger, full-color format!